YouTube Marketing Workbook: How to Use YouTube for Business

2016 Edition

by Jason McDonald, Ph.D.

© 2015-2016, JM Internet Group

https://www.jm-seo.org/

Tel. 800-298-4065

0

INTRODUCTION

Welcome to the *YouTube Marketing Workbook, 2016 edition*! Get ready to

- have some **fun**;
- **learn how YouTube works;**
- understand how to use **YouTube** to **market your business**; and
- create a step-by-step **YouTube marketing plan**.

Fully revised and updated for 2016, this workbook not only explains how to market on YouTube but also provides access to **free** YouTube marketing tools. It provides overviews, step-by-step instructions, tips and secrets, free tools for YouTube and video marketing, and (*wait, there's more!*) access to worksheets that will help you build a systematic YouTube / social media video marketing plan. Even better, if you register your copy, you also get access to my complete *Social Media Toolbook*, with literally hundreds of free social media marketing tools to turbocharge your social media marketing not just on YouTube but also on LinkedIn, Twitter, Facebook, Google+, Instagram and other major social media platforms.

> *It slices, it dices. It explains how to YouTube works. It gives you free tools. And it helps you make a YouTube marketing plan.*

If you're really gung-ho for **social media marketing**, I refer you to my *Social Media Workbook*, an all-in-one guide to the entire social media universe from YouTube to LinkedIn, Twitter to Facebook, Instagram to Pinterest, Yelp to Google+, and everything in between. Learn more about that book at http://jmlinks.com/social or call 800-298-4065.

Why Market via YouTube?

If you've read this far, you're definitely intrigued by YouTube as a marketing platform. Perhaps you're just starting out with a **YouTube Channel** for your **business**. Or perhaps you already have a Channel, but want to make it really work. Let's step back for a minute and ask: **why market on YouTube**?

Here are some reasons:

- **YouTube (and Video) are big.** YouTube is the second largest search engine, and video (of course) is increasingly dominant on the Internet.
- **YouTube is ubiquitous.** Nearly everyone uses YouTube – from teenagers to grandmas, business executives to flight attendants. YouTube – as we shall see – has three main uses: supportive, SEO, and sharing / viral. You don't have to be Rihanna or Miley Cyrus to benefit from YouTube!
- **YouTube is cheap**. YouTube is, of course, free to use. And in terms of marketing there is a lot you can do, for free, to build your brand, spread eWOM (electronic word of mouth), help you stay top-of-mind with your customers, and even "get shares" or "go viral." Google subsidizes YouTube, giving all of us free video hosting for our company videos.
- **YouTube has advertising.** If you advertise smart on YouTube, and combine paid advertising with free organic YouTube marketing, you can grow the reach of your company via video as well as use advertising to boost your organic YouTube performance.

YouTube, however, is also complicated. Using it is one thing, and marketing on YouTube is another. Most businesses fail at YouTube marketing because they just don't "get it." They don't understand how YouTube works, and they fail to see the incredible marketing opportunities beneath the surface of cat videos, Rihanna videos, and the latest video of Johnnie biting his finger. Quite simply, you have to invest some time to learn "how" to market on YouTube.

Enter the *YouTube Marketing Workbook*.

Who is this Workbook For?

This workbook is aimed primarily at **small business owners** and **marketing managers**. Non-profits will also find it useful.

If you are a person whose job involves advertising, marketing, and/or branding, this workbook is for you. If you are a small business that sees a marketing opportunity in

YouTube, this workbook is for you. And if your job is to market a business or organization online in today's Internet economy, this book is for you. Anyone who wants to look behind the curtain and understand the mechanics of how to market on YouTube will benefit from this book.

Anyone who sees – however dimly – that YouTube could help market their business will benefit from this hands-on guide.

How Does This Workbook Work?

This workbook starts first with an overview to **social media *marketing***. If social media is a **party**, then **using social media** is akin to just *showing up*. **Marketing** on social media, in contrast, isn't about showing up. It's about ***throwing*** the party!

Understanding that distinction between "attending" the social media party and "throwing" the social media party is the subject of **Chapter One.**

Chapter Two is a deep dive into YouTube marketing. We'll overview how YouTube works, explain everything from channels to videos, thumbs up to thumbs down, comments to shares, as well as the three uses of YouTube (supportive, SEO, and sharing). It will all become much clearer, as we work through YouTube in plain English, written for "mere mortals." Along the way, I'll provide **worksheets** that will act as "Jason as therapist," so you can fill them out and begin to outline your own unique YouTube marketing plan.

Finally, this workbook ends with an **Appendix**: a list of amazing **free YouTube tools** and resources. Even better, if you register your copy, you get clickable online access to the tools, a PDF copy of the book, and (wait, there's more!) a complimentary copy of my *Social Media Toolbook*, my compilation of hundreds of social media tools not just for YouTube but for all the major platforms.

Here's how to register your copy of this workbook:

1. Go to https://jm-seo.org/workbooks
2. Click on YouTube.
3. Use this password: **youtube2016**
4. You're in. Simply click on the link for a PDF copy of the *Social Media Toolbook* as well as access to the worksheets referenced herein.

OK, now that we know what this workbook is about, who it is for, and our plan of action...

Let's get started!

▶▶ MEET THE AUTHOR

My name is Jason McDonald, and I have been active on the Internet since 1994 (having invented the Internet along with Al Gore) and taught SEO, AdWords, and Social Media since 2009 – online, at Stanford University Continuing Studies, at both AcademyX and the Bay Area Video Coalition in San Francisco, at workshops, and in corporate trainings across these United States. I love figuring out how things work, and I love teaching others! Social media marketing is an endeavor that I understand, and I want to empower you to understand it as well.

Learn more about me at https://www.jasonmcdonald.org/ or at my corporate website https://www.jm-seo.org/. Or just call 800-298-4065, say something flattering, and I my secretary will put you through. *(Like I have a secretary! Just call if you have something to ask or say).*

▶▶ SPREAD THE WORD: WRITE A REVIEW & GET A FREE EBOOK!

If you like this workbook, please take a moment to write an honest review on Amazon.com. *If you hate the book, feel free to trash it on Amazon or anywhere across the Internet. (I have thick skin). If you hate life, in general, and are just one of those bitter people who write bitter reviews… well, gosh, go off and meditate, talk to a priest or do something spiritual. Life is just too short to be that bitter!*

At any rate, here is my special offer for those lively enough to write a review of the book–

1. Write your **honest review** on Amazon.com.
2. **Contact** me via https://www.jm-seo.org/contact and let me know your review is up.
3. Include your **email address** and **website URL**, and any quick questions you have about it.
4. I will send you a **free** copy of one of my other eBooks which cover AdWords, SEO, and Social Media Marketing.

This offer is limited to the first 100 reviewers, and only for reviewers who have purchased a paid copy of the book. You may be required to show proof of purchase and the birth certificate of your first born child, cat, or goldfish. If you don't have a child, cat, or goldfish, you may be required to prove telepathically that you bought the book.

▶▶ QUESTIONS AND MORE INFORMATION

I **encourage** my students to ask questions! If you have questions, submit them via https://www.jm-seo.org/contact/. There are two sorts of questions: ones that I know instantly, for which I'll zip you an email answer right away, and ones I do not know instantly, in which case I will investigate and we'll figure out the answer together.

As a teacher, I learn most from my students. So please don't be shy!

▶▶ COPYRIGHT AND DISCLAIMER

Uh! Legal stuff! Get ready for some fun:

Copyright © 2015-2016, JM Internet Group and Excerpti Communications, Inc., All Rights Reserved. No reproduction or citation without written consent of the publisher. For details and to contact us, visit our website at https://www.jm-seo.org/.

This is a completely **unofficial** guide to YouTube marketing. Neither YouTube nor Google has endorsed this guide, nor has anyone affiliated with YouTube or Google been involved in the production of this guide.

That's a *good thing*. This guide is **independent**. My aim is to "tell it as I see it," giving you no-nonsense information on how to succeed at YouTube marketing.

In addition, please note the following:

- All trademarks are the property of their respective owners. I have no relationship with nor endorsement from the mark holders. Any use of their marks is so I can provide information to you.

- Any reference to or citation of third party products or services whether for YouTube, LinkedIn, Twitter, Yelp, Google / Google+, Yahoo, Bing, Pinterest, Facebook, or other businesses, search engines, or social media platforms, should not be construed as an endorsement of those products or services tools, nor as a warranty as to their effectiveness or compliance with the terms of service with any search engine or social media platform.

The information used in this guide was derived in August, 2015. However, social media marketing changes rapidly, so please be aware that scenarios, facts, and conclusions are subject to change without notice.

Additional Disclaimer. Internet marketing is an art, and not a science. Any changes to your Internet marketing strategy, including SEO, Social Media Marketing, and AdWords, is at your own risk. Neither Jason McDonald, Excerpti Communications, Inc., nor the JM Internet Group assumes any responsibility for the effect of any changes you may, or may not, make to your website or AdWords advertising based on the information in this guide.

▶▶ ACKNOWLEDGEMENTS

No man is an island. I would like to thank my beloved wife, Noelle Decambra, for helping me hand-in-hand as the world's best moderator for our online classes, and as my personal cheerleader in the book industry. Gloria McNabb has done her usual tireless job as first assistant, including updating this edition as well the *Social Media Marketing* toolbook. Alex Facklis and Hannah McDonald also assisted with tools and research. I would also like to thank my black Labrador retriever, Buddy, for countless walks and games of fetch, during which I refined my ideas about marketing and about life.

And, again, a huge thank you to my students – online, in San Francisco, and at Stanford Continuing Studies. You challenge me, you inspire me, and you motivate me!

YouTube

YouTube (https://www.youtube.com/), in particular, and video in general, provide a two-for-one punch to your social media marketing. First, video itself can be the "there there," the content that you post to Twitter, Facebook, LinkedIn, etc. People love, watch, and share video as one of the most popular types of content across social media. Content is king, of course, and video content might even be considered the king of content. Second, beyond being content itself, YouTube is in and of itself a social media.

In this chapter, we'll explore video as content for social media. We'll also explore YouTube as a social media in its own right. You'll see similarities to Facebook: setting up a channel ("Page") on YouTube, uploading a video ("post") to YouTube, and the fact that people subscribe to your channel ("like" your "Page"). All of these dynamics are similar to Facebook. But video also brings three very different marketing mechanisms to the social media party: its use as a **supportive medium**, its use via **SEO** (Search Engine Optimization) to show at the top of Google and/or YouTube searches, and its use for **social sharing** or even **viral marketing**.

Let's get started!

To Do List:

» Explore how YouTube Works

» Inventory Companies on YouTube

» Set up Your Channel and Upload Videos

» Understand the Three Promotional Uses of Video

» Measure your Results

» Deliverable: a YouTube Marketing Plan

» Appendix: Top Ten YouTube Marketing Tools and Resources

» EXPLORE HOW YOUTUBE WORKS

Video and YouTube are among the most dramatic, most viral components of the Internet. Who doesn't know the "Harlem Shake" (http://jmlinks.com/1m) or the "Ice Bucket Challenge" (http://jmlinks.com/1n)? Who hasn't watched "Will it blend" (http://jmlinks.com/1o) or "Dear 16 Year Old Me" (http://jmlinks.com/1p)? And who hasn't fallen into the trap of assuming all YouTube is are silly cat videos, Rihanna videos, and inappropriate High School humor? It is, but YouTube is much, much more than that as a marketing opportunity (and as a social phenomenon).

As we shall see, there are three basic ways that YouTube videos can help you with social media marketing:

1. **Video as a supporting medium**: acting as the "content" that you "share" via other social media, including your website.
2. **Video as a discovery mechanism via SEO** (Search Engine Optimization), helping you promote your company, products, or services via search.
3. **Video as a share / viral promotion tactic**, because people love and share provocative videos.

We'll dive into the details in a moment. But first, log on to YouTube and get your bearings. (For the official YouTube starter guide, go to http://jmlinks.com/1q). If you're familiar with Facebook, you'll see many similarities right out of the gate:

- Individuals have an "account" or "**channel**" on YouTube, set up by registering with an email address and using Google+ to manage their account.
- Individuals can **upload videos** to their "channel," and when uploading give each video a TITLE, a DESCRIPTION, and KEYWORD TAGS as well as designate a VIDEO THUMBNAIL.
- Individuals "**subscribe**" to the channels of other individuals (or brands) on YouTube, and when someone you subscribe to uploads a new video, you get a

notification on your YouTube logon as well as via email that a new video has been posted.
- Individuals can **thumbs up / thumbs down videos** (akin to "like" on Facebook of a post), comment (via Google+ comments), and share the videos via other social media as well as create playlists of videos on YouTube.
- Companies can create **brand channels** on YouTube. Like Twitter, YouTube is very easy and open: anyone can quickly create a channel, no serious user authentication is required.

For assistance on how to set up a company YouTube channel, visit http://jmlinks.com/1r.

▶ INVENTORY COMPANIES ON YOUTUBE

After you've signed up for YouTube at least as an individual, your mission is to identify competitors on YouTube as well as brands you like in order to make an inventory of your likes and dislikes when it comes to YouTube as a channel for marketing.

How to Browse YouTube

One obvious way to make your short list of companies to follow is to simply visit their websites, and look for a link from their website to their YouTube channel. A big brand like REI (http://www.rei.com/), for example, will usually have the YouTube icon somewhere on the page: simply be signed into your personal YouTube account, click on their link to YouTube, and then once you land on their channel, click the red "subscribe" button.

A second way to find companies to subscribe to is to **browse YouTube**. When you are logged in to your YouTube account, simply click on the left hand side of the screen on "Browse channels."

There you'll see various subject-oriented groups of YouTube content, starting with *#PopularonYouTube*. On each category, you can click on the category name (e.g., *Film and Entertainment*), and drill down to channels in that category. Identify channels that interest you and hit the "subscribe" button. As you subscribe to channels, they will begin to appear on your home screen on the left column. To unsubscribe, just click on "Manage subscriptions" and/or go to the channel and hit the now-gray "Subscribed" button.

How to Search YouTube

Most of the action on YouTube really occurs at the level of the video, and not the channel. By this I mean that most of the high video counts, sharing, and even videos discovered via search occur via individual videos and not channels. You need to be a good searcher to understand YouTube!

To search YouTube directly, simply type keywords that matter to your company into the search bar at the top of the screen. For example type, *organic food*, to find YouTube videos on *organic food*. Like Google, YouTube will return a list of the most relevant videos. Simply click on a video to watch it, and then click "up" to the channel to learn more about the channel that produced it. Or you can just hit the red "Subscribe" button directly to subscribe to the channel. You can also thumb up / thumb down a video, comment on it (using your Google+ account), and share it. If you click on the share icon below a video, YouTube gives you all the social icons plus a link to "Embed," which provides the HTML code you need to embed a video on your own website or blog.

SEARCH YOUTUBE BY KEYWORDS TO FIND RELEVANT VIDEOS AND CHANNELS

Going back to search, type "organic food" into the search bar. Next, on the top left, click on "Filters," which opens up a set of parameters by which you can focus your search. Here's a screenshot:

Upload date	Type	Duration	Features	Sort by
Last hour	Video	Short (< 4 minutes)	4K	Relevance
Today	Channel	Long (> 20 minutes)	HD	Upload date
This week	Playlist		Subtitles/CC	View count
This month	Movie		Creative Commons	Rating
This year	Show		3D	
			Live	
			Purchased	
			360°	

Click *Upload date > This year*, which will turn on *filter #1* (videos of the last year), then reclick *filter*, and then click *Sort by > View Count*, which will turn on *filter #2* (most popular). In this way, you can find the most popular videos by view count vs. a time period (one year). You can also do this by week or month.

Remember: you are looking to understand what type of content is popular in your industry! Next click around at the various videos, and identify what sorts of topics you find people producing and watching in your industry. Pay attention to the thumbs up / thumbs down count, and comments per video. Like a good party planner, you are looking to identify the types of entertainment that attract and engage your guests.

With respect to an individual video, click on the "More" button underneath the video to see subscriptions driven and shares. By comparing one video to another, this data will help you understand not only what types of videos people like, but what types of videos cause them to take action: to subscribe to the channel and/or share the video with friends. Here's a screenshot of individual video data:

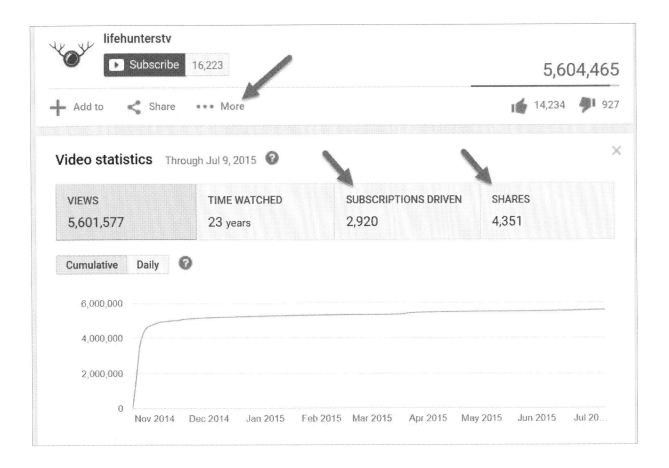

This means that this video had 5.6 million views, 14,234 thumbs ups, 927 thumbs down, drove 2,920 subscriptions to the channel, and had 4,351 shares via social media.

Competitor video data is hidden under the "more" button

You can gather this data, first, for competitor videos or videos that intrigue you to reverse engineer what works in terms of marketing via YouTube. Then, on your own videos, you can use this feature to see how well an individual video is performing.

Search Google for Videos

Another way to find interesting videos by keywords is to search Google. First type your keywords into Google, and then click the more > videos button. Here's a screenshot:

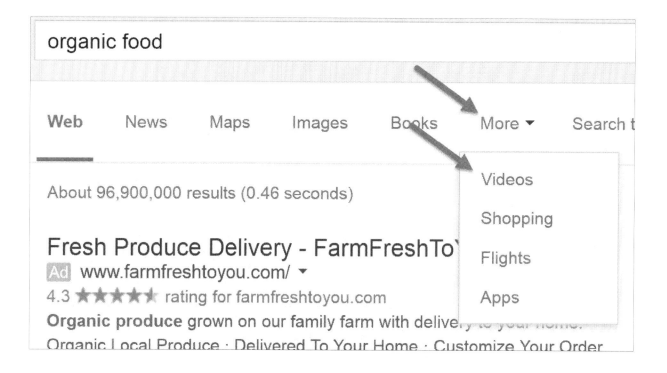

You can also use the button "Search Tools" to filter these results by videos of the last year, or by source (e.g., CNN.com or YouTube.com), but unlike on YouTube itself, you can't filter by view count.

By browsing, searching YouTube directly, or searching Google for videos, your objective is to identify videos that have high view counts as well as high thumbs up / thumbs down, comments, subscriptions driven, and share counts. What do people like? Why do they interact with it? How can this knowledge be applied to videos relevant to your company?

For your first **TODO**, download the **YouTube Research Worksheet**. For the worksheet, go to https://www.jm-seo.org/workbooks (click on YouTube, enter the code 'youtube2016' to register if you have not already done so), and click on the link to the "YouTube Research Worksheet." You'll answer questions as to whether your potential customers are on YouTube, identify brands to follow, and inventory what you like and dislike about their YouTube channels and individual videos.

❯❯ SET UP YOUR CHANNEL AND UPLOAD VIDEOS

After you've made an inventory of YouTube channels and videos that interest you from a marketing perspective, you're ready to set up your own YouTube channel. Assuming you haven't done this already, the best way to do this is from your Google+ account. Here are the steps:

1. **Login to your Google account** (either via Gmail or an email address for which you have created a Google account).
2. **Go to YouTube** by typing https://www.youtube.com/ in the browser address bar, or using the Google pull down menu to go to YouTube.
3. Under your name / icon on the top right, use the **pull down menu** and you will see a list of your associated Google+ company pages. Those that do not have a YouTube channel will have a gray message that says "create channel."
4. Click the **blue OK button**.

At that point, you will be "inside" your new YouTube channel. (If you already have a channel, simply login to YouTube.)

On the top right of the screen, click on your profile picture, and then **Creator Studio**. That gets you into the settings for your channel, as well as **video manager** (where you manage your videos). Click on "Community," where you can manage the ability of users to post comments to your video. Under "blacklist" you can also forbid the use of certain words, as well as ban users who have not behaved well from interacting with your channel.

To change your profile picture, click on your picture on the top right, hover over it, and click change. (Note that this will take you back to Google+; you'll have to return to YouTube to proceed.)

Click on *Channel*, on the left navigation. There are some basic set up and optimization tasks there, regarding how public your channel is, whether you allow advertising, etc. I do not recommend that you allow advertising or monetization on your channel, as your goal once you have a customer viewing your videos is for them to buy your product or service, not to go off and buy someone else's.

Furthermore, unless your view count is in the millions, you'll earn next to nothing via YouTube monetization. (The only practical reason to monetize a video is if you absolutely insist on using copyright-protected music; for that sort of music to be allowed, you must allow advertising on your video via monetization).

Next, click on the YouTube icon on the top left, and then My Channel. (*Confusingly, YouTube separates the Channel settings from the graphical look-and-feel of your channel*). As you hover over graphical elements, you'll see a tiny pencil. Click on the pencil and you can change and upload various elements.

- Hover and click the **pencil** to change your cover photo (called "Channel Art" in YouTube-speak).
- Click on the **About tab** to update information about your channel. At the bottom of this setting, you can create links to your other social media as well as your website.
- **Unsubscribed Trailer**. This is the YouTube name for the video that people see who are NOT subscribed to your channel. Think of it as a "Here's why you should subscribe video." It is often not enabled at first glance, so click on the pencil in the top right, then edit navigation, and then enable browse. (To watch a video explaining this visit http://jmlinks.com/1s).
  - Once this feature is enabled, you'll see a link "for new visitors" which sets the unsubscribed trailer and a link "for returning visitors" which sets what subscribers see.

Channel Optimization for SEO

YouTube is the No. 2 search engine, ahead of Bing (but behind its parent, Google). As I will discuss, you can optimize your YouTube videos for search by including relevant keywords. You should do the same with your channel. Place keywords in your channel keywords field. To enter your channel keywords, click on Creator Studio > Channel > Advanced > Channel keywords. Here's a screenshot:

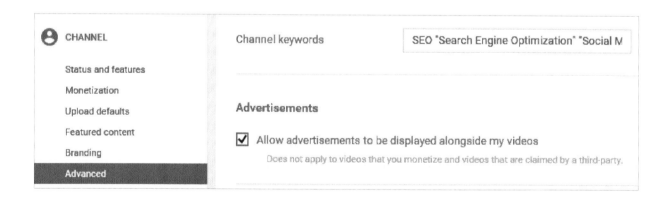

On the Advanced tag, you can also link your YouTube account to your AdWords account, as well as to your Google Analytics account for metrics purposes. Don't forget to associate your YouTube account with your website as well.

Click up to the "about" tab, and then click on the little pencil icon. Be sure to include logical search keywords in your company description on the "about" tab as well as links to your website and other social properties such as Twitter or Facebook.

Upload Videos

To upload a video, click back to your profile picture, then select "Creator Studio." Then on the right hand side click "Upload." Select a video to upload, and start uploading. As we will discuss below, input:

- **Video Title**: Write a keyword-heavy but catchy video title.
- **Description**. Write a keyword-heavy but catchy video description. Include an *http://www.yourcompany.com* link to your website. Be sure to use the http:// prefix, as that makes it "clickable" to your website.
- **Tags**. Identify no more than five relevant keywords tags for your video.
- **Public**: set the video to *public* (anyone can see), *unlisted* (only people with the link can view), or *private* (restricted access).
- **Custom thumbnail**. Upload a custom video thumbnail, which will appear in YouTube search. Or, YouTube will automatically create three options for you.

For your second Todo, download the **YouTube Setup Worksheet**. For the worksheet, go to https://www.jm-seo.org/workbooks (click on YouTube, enter the code 'youtube2016' to register if you have not already done so), and click on the link to the "YouTube Setup Worksheet." You'll answer and outline the basic setup issues for your YouTube channel.

» Understand the Three Promotional Uses of Video

While other social media have a posting strategy and posting rhythm, videos on YouTube are best understood by their three promotional strategies. While YouTube does have channels, subscriptions, and social spread just as other social media, the lion's share of activity comes directly from the videos themselves. Thus, it is very important to understand the three promotional uses of video.

YouTube Noise: Pop Culture

Before we turn to those uses of video, however, let's pause for a moment and consider the tremendous noise caused on YouTube by pop culture. When you innocently login to your YouTube account, you will be bombarded by a) music videos, b) ridiculous college humor / professional / silly videos, c) movie trailers, d) crazy trending news and so on and so forth. This is the dominant use of YouTube in terms of views, but just as cable TV has hundreds of channels and you can drill down to very specific, and very useful channels and programs (think, for example, about cooking or fishing shows on cable TV, that are not high volume but are very high value to people who really care about cooking or fishing). So, before your boss freaks about and dismisses YouTube because of the crazy videos on cats and the video by pop culture media icons, remember that for most of us marketers the value of YouTube is in the niches that matter to us: the niches that create and contain content that our customers care about. They exist: you just have to find them.

YouTube's pop culture hides productive niche uses of YouTube

Let's investigate the three basic uses of YouTube.

#1: Supportive Use of Video

If a picture is worth a thousand words, a video is worth ten thousand. If you are selling a complex product or service, creating and hosting explanatory videos can really help your sales process. Let's face it. Today's busy consumer doesn't really want to read a lot of text! They like videos because videos convey a lot of information quickly and easily, and videos convey emotional content.

Let's assume, for example, that you are a personal injury attorney in San Francisco. People are going to search for you via Google with keyword searches like "Personal Injury Attorneys SF," or "Auto Accident Attorney Bay Area." Then, they're going to land on your website, see a lot of intimidating text, and want to learn more about you as an attorney. Are you smart? Are you nice? Are you someone that they can trust?

In the old, pre-video days, they'd have to call you on the phone and come in for a quick interview. Then, they'd get in the car with their spouse, and have a little chat: *did you like her? Did she seem smart? Could we trust her with our case?* It would be all about "emotional intelligence," and "gut feeling."

Video allows you to post a quick introduction to you and/or your firm on your website, and start that process of "emotional intelligence" in just a few clicks of the mouse. In a very non-threatening way, videos give you the opportunity to pitch to a potential customer.

Here are some examples of this "supportive" use of video: videos that are not meant to "go viral," but rather to "support" the content of a website:

> **Mary Alexander Law** (http://www.maryalexanderlaw.com/). Notice the video right on the home page.
>
> **Sally Morin** (https://www.sallymorinlaw.com/). Ms. Morin produces a series of videos, again right on her home page.
>
> **Walkup Law** (http://www.walkuplawoffice.com/). Click on "watch our firm's approach."

Now, these videos may or may not be hosted on YouTube. That's not the point. The hosting location is not important: what's important is that in a complex industry such as legal services, these companies are using video to "support" the content of their website, and provide potential customers and "easy" way to acquire some "emotional intelligence" about the law firm.

Another area that uses videos in a supportive way is the technology industry. Take a look at the Analog Devices channel (https://www.youtube.com/user/AnalogDevicesInc). Watch a playlist of their videos from the Embedded World Trade Show at http://jmlinks.com/1t. Essentially, they are taking a video recorder to the trade show, and recording the "dog and pony show" that each product marketing engineer gives to a prospect who walks up to the trade show booth. The dance goes like this:

- *Hi, what does Analog Devices have new and exciting for engineers that you're exhibiting at the Embedded World Trade show?*
- *Oh, hi there, my name is John Doe, Product Marketing Manager at Analog Devices of the super widget. Let me walk you through what we're exhibiting.*

> *Thank you. (Mentally: oh that's interesting, that fits what I need, he seems like a nice guy, and they seem like a great company... I'll follow up on doing business together after the show).*

By posting these videos to YouTube, Analog Devices creates linkable, sharable **content**, that it can post to its Facebook, Twitter, LinkedIn, and even website pages. It can also email these videos out to prospective clients who inquire but were unable to attend the industry trade show. They are using video to ***support*** their marketing efforts, and none of these videos are designed to "go viral" like a cat video or Rihanna's latest over-the-top music video. That's not their purpose.

A third way to see the supportive use of video is to go to Facebook, and look at brands you admire. You'll often see them sharing video content. Use a tool like Buzzsumo (http://www.buzzsumo.com/), enter your keywords, and look for videos that are being shared on social media. In most cases, these videos are functioning to "support" the social media marketing: like blog posts, videos can be simply content that you share.

If you sell something complex, something that people use "emotional intelligence" to evaluate, video allows you the opportunity to share that information quickly and easily. If you have "how to" content that is best explained visually, videos can be fantastic for your social media marketing. Any type of content that is better explained by "showing" than by "writing" is an excellent candidate for video. You can also, of course, use video for "after the sale" events such explanations to commonly asked technical support questions.

The supportive use of video, with free hosting of those videos on YouTube and a universal player, is not an opportunity to be missed!

#2: Search Discovery or SEO Use of Video

YouTube is the No. two search engine, behind Google and far ahead of Bing. One of the heaviest uses of YouTube is for "how to" searches. Simply go to YouTube and start typing "how to" and you'll see a list of common YouTube searches.

Here's a screenshot:

```
how to
how to make five nights at freddy's not scary
how to tie a tie
how to draw
how to get a six pack in 3 minutes
how to basic
how to make a paper gun that shoots
how to save a life
how to download youtube video
how to whip
how to draw a rose
```

If you're company has any type of "how to" content, especially "how to" content that is best explained in a visual way, you can SEO-optimize YouTube videos to show up for search.

Let's say, for example, that you sell pet food. People who have new puppies are often curious about how best to feed their new puppy. So they'll Google or search via YouTube "How to feed a puppy." Presto! You know have an idea for an informative video, and in that video you can embed mentions, and links to your website for more information and products to buy. Or let's say that you sell makeup. People are dying to know the best way to put on mascara. So they search "How to put on Mascara." Here's a screenshot of common "how to" searches with makeup:

```
how to put on
how to put on fake eyelashes
how to put on eyeliner
how to put on makeup for beginners
how to put on makeup
how to put on eyeshadow
how to put on a tampon
how to put on a tie
how to put on lipstick
how to put on a wig
how to put on mascara
```

So your first step is to do some keyword research. What types of searches are people making on YouTube that are relevant to your product or service? Use "YouTube suggest" by simply typing keywords into YouTube and paying attention to what people enter (this is driven, largely, by keyword search volume). Use a tool like Ubersuggest (http://ubersuggest.org/) which will pull all the "suggestions" from Google. And use the Google keyword planner tool (http://jmlinks.com/1u) to identify high volume, high value keyword searches on Google (which generally also translate to YouTube). For a video on how to use the Google Keyword Planner, visit http://jmlinks.com/1v.

As for keywords, also pay attention to very specific branded searches. If a competitor has a hard-to-use product, and you know that people search YouTube for that product, you can include that product name in your video headline, to snag viewers who are searching for the product. Identify adjacent, branded search terms and snag that traffic to your own videos. For example, a YouTube search such as "Netgear router set up" or "How to use a Black and Decker drill" are ripe for this type of adjacent keyword optimization.

Once you've identified keywords that people search on Google and/or YouTube, looking for video content, it's time to optimize your video using that tactics of Search Engine Optimization or SEO. Here's what to do:

1. **Create Your Video**. Obviously, you have to create a short, informative video that explains "how to" do what people are looking to understand. It should be primarily informative, but showcase your product or service nonetheless.
2. **Optimize the Video Title**. Write a keyword-heavy video title.
3. **Optimize the Video Description**. Write a keyword-heavy video description and include a link in http:// format to your website for more information.
4. **Optimize the Video Transcript**. YouTube pays attention to what you "say" in the video via voice recognition software, so be sure to "say" the keywords when you are presenting. For example, "In this video, I am going to explain how to tie a tie."
5. **Optimize the Video Tags**. When you upload the video, be sure to use no more than five keyword-relevant tags.

Important. It's a best practice to have your keyword-heavy content ready to go upon upload, as the first indexing by YouTube is the strongest. Don't upload first in a temporary version, and come back later to optimize.

Take a look at some of these "how to" searches, and browse the top-ranked videos to confirm how they optimize their video titles and descriptions:

- How to Put on Eyeliner at http://jmlinks.com/1w
- How to stop a puppy from chewing on a leash at http://jmlinks.com/1x
- Living wills and advanced directives at http://jmlinks.com/1y.

It's easy to optimize the video headline, description, and tags (not visible to the user). That's your first step.

Next, you need to think about **interactivity**. In rewarding videos with top search positions, YouTube pays a lot of attention to how many views a video has and how interactive a video is, similar to the way that Facebook rewards posts that have high Edgerank. You want users to "interact" with your video: thumbs up / thumbs down, comment, share, and embed. How do you get that?

- **Ask.** In your video, ask users to "subscribe to your channel," or "thumbs up" if you like the video, or "enter questions in the comments below." You can drive interactivity simply by asking for it.

- **Annotations.** Use annotations (text messages) on the top of the video to promote interactivity. In YouTube's Video Manager, click on a video, and then click on "Annotations" in the top row.

Here's a screenshot of annotations:

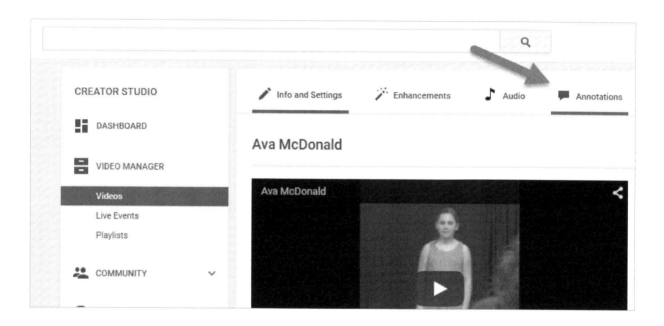

You can create clickable links to other videos as well as to the subscribe feature, and you can create messages to users that ask for interactivity.

Overlays on YouTube

Also, by advertising on YouTube (with a minimum budget of just a dollar or less per day), you can put clickable *YouTube overlays* on your videos. *These overlays show on the video on all times, including when it is being viewed or found organically.* To set up an overlay, first turn "on" advertising on AdWords. Then create a "video ad" for your video. Next, fill in the overlay information. Finally, set a very low budget such as $1.00 per day per 10 videos. Presto! All of your video views, including those that originate from organic (non-advertising) searches, will have overlays. In short, once a video is being advertised via Google AdWords, the overlay function is turned on, *regardless of how small the budget being spent.*

Third, you'll need to think about external **promotion**. Since YouTube pays attention to the **view count** (*higher is better*) as well as interactivity, use your other social networks to promote your video. Post your video to Facebook, Twitter, LinkedIn, etc., email your video link out to your email link. Even consider advertising the video upon launch on YouTube (http://www.youtube.com/yt/advertise/), to drive the view count up as well as the interactions. "Embeds" of your video (when your video is embedded or linked to from an external website) are also important to drive a video to the top of search. The more views of your video, the more embeds of your video across the Web, the higher it will rank in relevant YouTube and Google searches.

CREATE A VIRTUOUS CIRCLE: THE MORE A VIDEO IS VIEWED, THE MORE IT SHOWS IN SEARCH

The on page text optimization of the video, interactivity, and external promotion all drive a video to the top of YouTube. Once on the top of YouTube search, a **virtuous circle** can kick in: the more it shows at the top of YouTube search, the more people watch it, the more they watch it, the higher the view count and interactivity, which drives it higher on search and so on and so forth.

#2: Sharing and Viral Videos

Videos are one of the most shared content across social media. We've all seen compelling videos, and shared them across Facebook, Twitter, or LinkedIn. Videos are highly shareable! Why? Largely because video can convey emotional content in a much easier way than can text or images. And emotion drives sharing: funny, shocking, provocative, outrageous – any of the big human emotions are the ultimate driver of sharing across social media.

VIDEOS GET SHARED BECAUSE OF EMOTIONAL CONTENT

If you have a product or service that people do not heavily search for, then you can attempt to leverage the share path via YouTube. How? First and foremost, identify a logical **emotion** to drive the shares. Utility is one emotion, in the sense that people will share a video that is useful with friends of family. For example, a video on "how to make your Facebook completely private" (http://jmlinks.com/1z) has over 500,000 views. So creating something so useful that people share it with friends and family is one way to leverage YouTube sharing to promote your product.

But utility is the weakest of human emotions. **Fear, anger, outrage, humor** – all of these emotions are much, much stronger than mere utility!

For most businesses, the best emotion to tap is **humor**, because humor can encourage sharing without having negative side effects on your brand image. One business that has really leveraged YouTube sharing is Blendtec Blenders (http://www.blendtec.com/). Their YouTube channel, entitled, "Will it blend" (https://www.youtube.com/user/Blendtec) is all about taking crazy items and blending them in their powerful blenders: being humorous and yet showcasing their product. One of my favorite viral videos produced by Blendtec concerns Justin Bieber, with over 3.4 million views. Watch it at http://jmlinks.com/2a.

If you can connect your product to something insanely funny, then you can use humor as the "fuel" to drive social sharing of your product or service. Just remember it has to be insanely funny. Other examples are "Girls don't poop" (http://jmlinks.com/2b) or "The man your man could smell like" (http://jmlinks.com/2c). For the latter, I recommend you read the Wikipedia discussion at http://jmlinks.com/2d, where you'll learn that "behind the scenes" an immense amount of work and promotion went on to make the video "go viral."

Going Viral

To "go viral," a video must be so highly shared that one person shares it with two, and the two share it with four and so on and so forth. For a video to go viral, it must have strong emotional pull, and to get started, must usually have strong external promotion including advertising.

It takes a match to ignite a forest fire, after all.

Humor is one emotion that can start viral sharing. Another is **sentimentality**. Especially for non-profits, videos that tug on the emotions can be used to encourage social sharing. Examples of this strategy are "Dear 16 Year Old Me" (http://jmlinks.com/1p) and "Dear Future Mom" (http://jmlinks.com/2e). These videos feature real people, sharing authentic emotional stories about a social cause or problem.

People share them to "support" the cause. The "Ice bucket challenge" and "It gets better" are other example of this use of "showing support" to promote a cause.

Finally, I want to draw your attention to Mike Tompkins (https://www.youtube.com/user/pbpproductions) as an example of a marketer who leverages viral sharing via YouTube. Tompkins produces "covers" of pop songs on YouTube, such as his first on Miley Cyrus "Party in the USA" (http://jmlinks.com/2f). The strategy is to "piggy back" on popular YouTube searches for "branded content" (e.g., "Party in the USA" or "Party in the USA cover") and then "hijack" users to his own wonderful videos. Then, users "subscribe" to his channel, and he has a promotional vehicle combining YouTube search and viral sharing, because his videos are strong and innovative enough to be shareable in their own right.

It's not search OR share on YouTube: it's search AND share.

Indeed a video such as Tompkins' "Starships" (http://jmlinks.com/2g) is leveraging search, share, and the use of influencers (the cast of Pitch Perfect) to promote it and get it to "go viral"). Similarly, the "It gets better project" (http://www.itgetsbetter.org/) is leveraging influencers, sentimentality, user generated content, and a "cause" that many people agree with to get its videos to "go viral" and spread its message.

As a marketer, the task is to "reverse engineer" these efforts at sharing and virality and determine if there is a path to viral marketing that fits your company. Again, for most for-profit companies, the best emotion is humor, while for many non-profits, sentimentality and causes that people actively support are good mechanisms to spur social sharing.

To summarize, brainstorm which of the following uses of YouTube are most relevant for your company:

> **Supportive.** Create and upload videos that support your website and other social media. This is largely using YouTube as a hosting platform as opposed to a promotional system.
>
> **Search / SEO.** To the extent that people search for keywords near your product or service, you can optimize your videos for discovery by search.
>
> **Share / Viral.** To the extent that your videos have an emotional content, you can encourage discovery by social sharing and even virality.

Remember that in all cases you usually need to use external promotion tactics such as sharing your videos on Facebook, Twitter, and LinkedIn, reaching out to influencers who will help promote your videos, and even advertising on YouTube to extend the reach of your videos.

▶▶ MEASURE YOUR RESULTS

Owned by Google, YouTube provides very good metrics on both your channel and your videos. From insider your YouTube account, click on *Creator Studio > Analytics*. Next, you can drill down to any video, and investigate:

> **Views.** Total views and views over time.
>
> **Estimated Minutes Watched.** Total minutes watched.
>
> **Engagement.** Variables such as likes, dislikes, comments, shares, videos in playlists, and subscribers generated by the video.
>
> **Demographics.** Your top countries and gender distribution.
>
> **Discovery.** How people found your video. Click into "top traffic sources" to view the actual search keywords, "external" to view referrer websites, "suggested videos" to view related videos that generated traffic

You can also manage your user comments from insider Creator Studio. Click on Community > Comments to view, respond, and even delete comments from users.

Google Analytics

For many of us, we want to drive traffic from YouTube to our website, even to our ecommerce store or to download a free eBook or software package to get a sales lead. Sign up for Google Analytics (https://www.google.com/analytics) and install the required tracking code. Inside of your Google Analytics account on the left column, drill down by clicking on *Acquisition > Social > Overview*. Then on the right hand side of the screen you'll see the word "Social." Click on that, and then find YouTube on the list, and YouTube to your Website, giving you insights into what types of video people find attractive.

You can also create a custom Advanced Segment to look at only YouTube traffic and its behavior. For information on how to create custom Advanced Segments in Google Analytics, go to http://jmlinks.com/1f. For the Google help files on Advanced Segments go to http://jmlinks.com/1g.

In sum, inside of YouTube you can see how people interact with your channel and videos. Inside of Google Analytics, you can see where they land on your website and what they do after they arrive.

» DELIVERABLE: A YOUTUBE MARKETING PLAN

Now that we've come to the end of our chapter on YouTube, your **DELIVERABLE** has arrived. Go to https://www.jm-seo.org/workbooks (click on YouTube, enter the code 'youtube2016' to register if you have not already done so), and click on the link to the "YouTube Marketing Plan." By filling out this plan, you and your team will establish a vision of what you want to achieve via YouTube.

» APPENDIX: TOP TEN YOUTUBE MARKETING TOOLS AND RESOURCES

Here are the top ten tools and resources to help you with YouTube marketing. For an up-to-date list, go to https://www.jm-seo.org/workbooks (click on YouTube, enter the code 'youtube2016' to register if you have not already done so). Click on the *Social Media Toolbook* link, and drill down to the YouTube chapter.

YOUTUBE TOOLS - http://youtube.com/yt/creators/tools.html

> YouTube has done more and more to make it easier to publish and promote videos. This page lists six tools: YouTube Capture, YouTube Editor, Captions, Audio Library, Slideshow and YouTube Analytics. All of them are fantastic, free tools about YouTube by YouTube.
>
> **Rating:** 5 Stars | **Category:** resource

YOUTUBE CREATOR HUB - http://youtube.com/yt/creators

> Help center for those creating YouTube content. Learn how to better edit your videos, get them up on YouTube, etc. Has lessons on growing your audience, boot camp, and how to get viewers and even how to earn money via YouTube.

Rating: 5 Stars | **Category:** resource

YOUTUBE ADVERTISING GUIDE - http://youtube.com/yt/advertise/index.html

This can be buried, and hard to find - leave it to the folks at Google and YouTube. But this is the scoop on how (and why) to advertise on YouTube.

Rating: 4 Stars | **Category:** overview

YOUTUBE HELP CENTER - http://support.google.com/youtube

The official help site for YouTube, conveniently located on Google. Google owns YouTube, but you already knew that.

Rating: 4 Stars | **Category:** overview

YOUTUBE CAPTURE - https://youtube.com/capture

YouTube Capture is an app for your mobile phone, which makes it easy to capture and edit videos right on your phone. Imagine you are a marketer / retailer and you want to use your phone to easily capture customer interactions, and upload (quickly / easily) to YouTube. Get the picture?

Rating: 4 Stars | **Category:** tool

YOUTUBE CREATOR ACADEMY - http://creatoracademy.withgoogle.com

Learn tips and tricks from the YouTube pros to maximize your corporate YouTube page. Expert videos, tests, and even a way to 'meet' other YouTube content creators. Fun, friendly, and free.

Rating: 3 Stars | **Category:** resource

TUBECHOP - http://tubechop.com

Enter a YouTube video URL, watch it, and 'chop it' at the moment you want a user to see. This way, you can share just the portion of a video you want, rather than forcing people to watch a long boring intro or other non-relevant content.

Rating: 3 Stars | **Category:** tool

YouTube Help Channel - https://youtube.com/youtubehelp

More for general users than for marketers, the YouTube Help channel has informative videos on how to 'use' YouTube. That said, if you know how your customers use YouTube, you can become a better marketer towards them. Includes tutorials, troubleshooting, and tips. Never stop learning!

Rating: 3 Stars | **Category:** resource

YouTube Creator Studio Android App - http://bit.ly/1dqVLc2

Use YouTube Creator Studio to manage your channel from your Android phone. Great when you're on the go. For iTunes version go to http://bit.ly/yc-iphone.

Rating: 3 Stars | **Category:** tool

YouTube Editor - https://youtube.com/editor

While there is Microsoft Windows Movie Maker and Apple iMovie, there is also a free YouTube editor for your videos. Not incredibly powerful, but free and easy to use 'in the cloud.'

Rating: 3 Stars | **Category:** tool

YOUTUBE TOOLS

YouTube, like all social media, has a cornucopia of free resources and free tools to make your life easier. Below I produce my favorite tools and resources (in rank order). Remember that by registering your copy of the workbook, you can access the *Social Media Toolbook*, which has all the tools in convenient, clickable PDF format. To register, go to https://www.jm-seo.org/workbooks (click on YouTube, enter the code 'youtube2016' to register if you have not already done so), and click on the link to the *Social Media Toolbook*.

Here are free YouTube tools and resources, sorted with the best items first.

YOUTUBE TOOLS - http://youtube.com/yt/creators/tools.html

YouTube has done more and more to make it easier to publish and promote videos. This page lists six tools: YouTube Capture, YouTube Editor, Captions, Audio Library, Slideshow and YouTube Analytics. All of them are fantastic, free tools about YouTube by YouTube.

Rating: 5 Stars | **Category:** resource

VIRAL VIDEO CHART - http://viralvideochart.unrulymedia.com/all

See what videos are going viral on YouTube right now. Enter your KEYWORDS in search box at TOP RIGHT to see what videos people are SHARING in your industry. Very cool and fun!

Rating: 5 Stars | **Category:** service

An Advertiser's Guide to YouTube - http://youtube.com/watch?v=n-q5zZ1p2eM

With YouTube there is finally a way to reach that niche market known as 'everybody'. Watch this video to understand the basics of advertising on YouTube. This is YouTtube's pitch about advertising directly on YouTube. Unlike the Google ads, it isn't boring. It's fun to watch!

Rating: 5 Stars | **Category:** video

YouTube Creator Hub - http://youtube.com/yt/creators

Help center for those creating YouTube content. Learn how to better edit your videos, get them up on YouTube, etc. Has lessons on growing your audience, boot camp, and how to get viewers and even how to earn money via YouTube.

Rating: 5 Stars | **Category:** resource

YouTube Advertising Guide - http://youtube.com/yt/advertise/index.html

This can be buried, and hard to find - leave it to the folks at Google and YouTube. But this is the scoop on how (and why) to advertise on YouTube.

Rating: 4 Stars | **Category:** overview

ReelSEO Video Marketer's Guide - http://reelseo.com

A leading resource for news, analysis, tips and trends for the online video and Internet marketing industries. Their videologists and columnists offer expert advice, guidance, and commentary about the world of online video to guide Internet marketers and video content producers on best practices and online video services that suit their needs.

Rating: 4 Stars | **Category:** portal

Small Business Guide to YouTube - http://simplybusiness.co.uk/microsites/youtube-for-small-business

Interactive step-by-step flowchart to YouTube marketing. Comprised of key questions and linked resources with more information. Excellent resource. Worth a look.

Rating: 4 Stars | **Category:** resource

YOUTUBE HELP CENTER - http://support.google.com/youtube

The official help site for YouTube, conveniently located on Google. Google owns YouTube, but you already knew that.

Rating: 4 Stars | **Category:** overview

YOUTUBE SPOTLIGHT - http://youtube.com/youtube

Trying to understand YouTube? This is the official YouTube Channel by YouTube on YouTube. Use to to discover what's new and trending around the world from music to culture to Internet phenomena, must-watch videos from across YouTube, all in one place.

Rating: 4 Stars | **Category:** video

YOUTUBE CAPTURE - https://youtube.com/capture

YouTube Capture is an app for your mobile phone, which makes it easy to capture and edit videos right on your phone. Imagine you are a marketer / retailer and you want to use your phone to easily capture customer interactions, and upload (quickly / easily) to YouTube. Get the picture?

Rating: 4 Stars | **Category:** tool

YOUTUBE ADVERTISING RESOURCES - https://youtube.com/yt/advertise/resources.html

YouTube wants you to advertise! But, it also hides some good free SEO-oriented resources here for how to use YouTube effectively. Worth a look, and a bookmark.

Rating: 4 Stars | **Category:** resource

iMovie for Mac - https://apple.com/mac/imovie

Apple's free, downloadable movie / video editor. Great for making YouTube videos!

Rating: 4 Stars | **Category:** tool

Popular on YouTube - https://www.youtube.com/channel/UCF0pVplsI8R5kcAqgtoRqoA

An auto-generated collection of what's popular on YouTube, and - shall we say - 'going viral.' As a marketer, seek to observe and understand why things go viral and how to leverage the video popularity wave.

Rating: 4 Stars | **Category:** service

YouTube Trends Dashboard - http://youtube.com/trendsdashboard

Find out what's trending on YouTube. Trend search on YouTube. Get some viral video ideas.

Rating: 3 Stars | **Category:** tool

YouTube Creator Academy - http://creatoracademy.withgoogle.com

Learn tips and tricks from the YouTube pros to maximize your corporate YouTube page. Expert videos, tests, and even a way to 'meet' other YouTube content creators. Fun, friendly, and free.

Rating: 3 Stars | **Category:** resource

YouTube Help Forum - http://productforums.google.com/forum/#!forum/youtube

The new and improved forum by and about YouTube - user-generated content, helpful tips and pointers from official YouTubers. This is your 'goto' site if you want to post a question for the community and hopefully get some help.

Rating: 3 Stars | **Category:** resource

TubeChop - http://tubechop.com

Enter a YouTube video URL, watch it, and 'chop it' at the moment you want a user to see. This way, you can share just the portion of a video you want, rather than forcing people to watch a long boring intro or other non-relevant content.

Rating: 3 Stars | **Category:** tool

YouTube Help Channel - https://youtube.com/youtubehelp

More for general users than for marketers, the YouTube Help channel has informative videos on how to 'use' YouTube. That said, if you know how your customers use YouTube, you can become a better marketer towards them. Includes tutorials, troubleshooting, and tips. Never stop learning!

Rating: 3 Stars | **Category:** resource

YouTube Creator Studio Android App - http://bit.ly/1dqVLc2

Use YouTube Creator Studio to manage your channel from your Android phone. Great when you're on the go. For iTunes version go to http://bit.ly/yc-iphone.

Rating: 3 Stars | **Category:** tool

Windows Movie Maker - http://windows.microsoft.com/en-us/windows-live/movie-maker

For those on the Windows platform, Movie Maker is the goto free program to edit videos for YouTube and other platforms.

Rating: 3 Stars | **Category:** tool

YouTube Facebook Page - https://facebook.com/youtube

YouTube is on Facebook. So if you love YouTube and you love Facebook, you'll love YouTube on Facebook - keep up with the latest trends.

Rating: 3 Stars | **Category:** resource

YouTube Advertisers Channel - https://youtube.com/user/advertise

Interested in advertising on YouTube? This is the official channel with tons of useful, if salesy, content on why and how to advertise your products or services on YouTube. If you're into advertising, check out the 'Ads Leaderboard,' which highlights top ads month by month.

Rating: 3 Stars | **Category:** video

YouTube Creators Blog - http://youtubecreator.blogspot.com

The official YouTube blog by and about YouTube partners. You can pick up some good tips on YouTube marketing here, plus learn some ins and outs from YouTube superstars. Plus it's just plain fun to see what the YouTube famous are up to.

Rating: 3 Stars | **Category:** blog

YouTube Editor - https://youtube.com/editor

While there is Microsoft Windows Movie Maker and Apple iMovie, there is also a free YouTube editor for your videos. Not incredibly powerful, but free and easy to use 'in the cloud.'

Rating: 3 Stars | **Category:** tool

YouTube Blog - http://youtube-global.blogspot.com

The official YouTube blog. If YouTube is important to you - whether as a video hosting service and/or as a social media method to connect with customers - here is where you find the inside scoop on Google's YouTube service.

Rating: 3 Stars | **Category:** blog

Wideo - http://wideo.co

An online video maker, similar to iMovie or Windows Movie Maker.

Rating: 3 Stars | **Category:** tool

YOUTUBE (BRAND) CHANNELS - https://support.google.com/youtube/topic/4601639

Brand channels on YouTube have an advertising component, but many of the items on this page are applicable to regular channels on YouTube as well. So this is a useful 'how to' article on managing a brand page on YouTube.

Rating: 2 Stars | **Category:** article

POWTOON - https://powtoon.com

PowToon provides animated video production using the freemium pricing model. Play around with it to create animated videos to present anything you want about your business. Paid plans available, but you can do some cool stuff for free.

Rating: 2 Stars | **Category:** tool

YOUTUBE ON TWITTER - https://twitter.com/youtube

YouTube's official Twitter profile (@YouTube). So does Twitter have an official channel on YouTube? This could get weird.

Rating: 2 Stars | **Category:** resource

TRENDING ON YOUTUBE - http://google.com/trends/hotvideos

The wild, wild, wild world of YouTube as told by Google Trends. See what's trending on YouTube. Unfortunately, you can't zoom in, manage, change, or do anything. Google, in its infinite wisdom only lets you see what it wants you to see: mass market trends on YouTube. Still, it's fun (and annoying, and revealing, and funny, and depressing).

Rating: 2 Stars | **Category:** service

GOOGLE YOUTUBE CHANNELS DIRECTORY - https://www.google.com/press/youtube-directory.html

Directory of all the official Google channels on YouTube. So if you want to find out if Google Analytics has an official YouTube channel, this is a good place to start.

Rating: 1 Stars | **Category:** resource

YOUTUBE ON GOOGLE+ - https://plus.google.com/+youtube

If you are really into YouTube, follow them on social media. Here is their Google+ page.

Rating: 1 Stars | **Category:** resource

YOUTUBE TRENDS BLOG - http://youtube-trends.blogspot.com

YouTube reflects and sets trends. This is their blog and service to help identify trends on YouTube.

Rating: 1 Stars | **Category:** blog

Printed in Great Britain
by Amazon